Survival Foods To Stockpile: Emergency Prepping Guide For Life-Saving Supplies And Food Storage

Pandemic Survival, Volume 5

Mary White

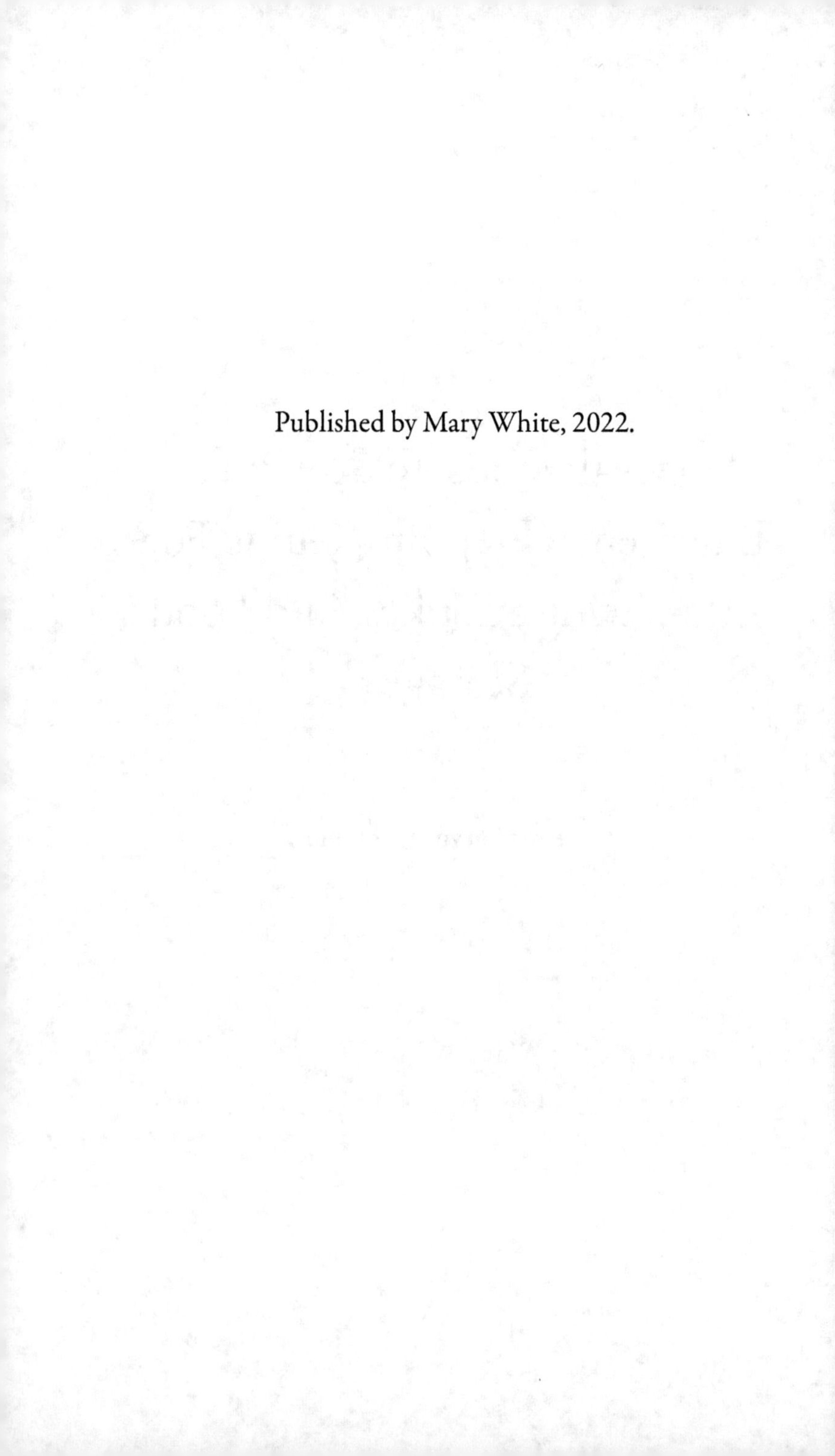

Published by Mary White, 2022.

While every precaution has been taken in the preparation of this book, the publisher assumes no responsibility for errors or omissions, or for damages resulting from the use of the information contained herein.

SURVIVAL FOODS TO STOCKPILE: EMERGENCY PREPPING GUIDE FOR LIFE-SAVING SUPPLIES AND FOOD STORAGE

First edition. February 22, 2022.

Copyright © 2022 Mary White.

ISBN: 979-8201495435

Written by Mary White.

Survival Foods To Stockpile

Mary White

1

whether directly or indirectly, of any advice or information presented, whether for breach of contract, tort, negligence, personal injury, criminal intent, or under any other cause of action.

You agree to accept all risks of using the information presented inside this book.

You agree that by continuing to read this book, where appropriate and/or necessary, you shall consult a professional (including but not limited to your doctor, attorney, or financial advisor or such other advisor as needed) before using any of the suggested remedies, techniques, or information in this book.

Introduction

Whether you want to be prepared for the end of the world as we know it or just a financial collapse, it's always a good idea to be prepared. It is known that at least 3 to 4 million people in the US are prepping for some kind of catastrophe. It would stand to reason the number is very much higher, due to the fact that a lot of people are afraid of what others may think. After doing the research, the number of people that seem to think that, that type of preparation is needed is more like 50%. Does this seem odd? When questioning real people, it seems to hold up. All those folks do not and don't plan on actually doing any prep, but are thinking there may come a time when the lack of prep would have been a mistake.

It's obvious nowadays that stability in our society is suspect at best. Being prepared is starting to become a common theme. Especially when people are now starting to realize that bad things can and do happen and no timely response may be seen when it does happen. It's well known now that QE (Quantitative Easing) is causing the rich to get richer and the not so well off to join the lower income class or no income class. Because of that, possible financial collapse is a concern. Conflicts and natural disasters are another great concern. Our population could be on its way to possible disaster.

When a person sees, this may happen to themselves and their family and friends, the obvious response is to prepare for the worst. A sense of protection is natural for themselves and those whom they care about. Many people don't act on this knowledge, but a large number of people are, a very large number. This has spawned a wide variety of prepper types. Some prepare for short term problems, while others prepare for many years of protection. It would seem that the ones who prepare for the long term are making the best move, considering the world environment. When you consider what the government seems to have been doing in recent years. Mass preparation for something big, messy, and that covers a very long time period seems to be taking place. To deny this overlooks the obvious. Everybody knows that when there is a problem, they will protect themselves first and you may never see a response to your situation. That fear is enough for almost anyone to consider and enact some type of prepper plan.

There seems to be one type of common mistake though. Many people get the idea its okay to prep at home and let others know about it. They overlook the obvious truth. All homes will be a target for food and supplies, whether preppers are there or not. Not only is it good to have a location that doesn't look like a home with goods in it, but complete secrecy about what you are doing is a must, not at prepper conventions where you are basically anonymous, but with people who can organize and find you when there is a real problem. Unfortunately, even family members whom you normally trust and want to protect in a disaster are high risk for telling others. That means it's better to make sure you know where they are and have the means to go get them when the time comes. That may involve a well-protected form of travel, weapons and a network of others like you that you trust to retrieve and deliver someone to you if you are unable to travel.

This would include a good form of uninterruptible communication with that group of people using a method such as a shortwave (Ham) radio system. Nowadays this form of communication can be bought in a small hand-held form. That unit should be able to connect to an auxiliary antenna if needed. Though more power would be needed, such as with a base unit, for worldwide communication, the low power hand held unit would be great for long distance local use. Everybody should understand that cell phones should never be counted on to be up and running in a real disaster situation. They can however be rigged, with proper software, to allow for restricted distance communication with another phone. This would be "off system" walkie talkie type 2-way communication. This type of communication can also be encrypted between phones so that the conversations can't be monitored. This type of hack would take place after the traditional system became non-operational or was suspect that big brother may be listening in.

Unfortunately, many preppers are just setting themselves up to be raided or robbed by others wishing to obtain their goods by not following these obvious tips to maintain secrecy. The government may raid you if they feel you are not conforming to their new idea of what you should be doing with your hoard or what orders you should be following given by them to the general public, if they know where you are and can enforce those new rules. If it is not obvious where you are and you are not showing outward signs at your location that you are there or need to be investigated, chances are you can wait out the disaster until the proper outside environment exists. If you have the correct supplies to do so. It is usually better to be under your own self-imposed restrictions than someone else's and not be out of your comfort and supplies zone.

Intelligence is strength. The phase, only the strong survive applies to how intelligent you are and what you do with that intelligence to protect yourself and others you care about. It is your responsibility to take the correct steps or not be able to care for yourself and others when the time comes. Just like how people plan in normal life, they should plan for abnormal life. Those who don't are not as intelligent as those who do, liked or not, the fact still remains. Anyone who is not aware of the risks around them and then not properly plan for those risks, are not acting in an intelligent manner, whether they think they are smart or not. It makes no sense that communities don't have designated protection areas with proper supplies for their citizens anymore. Grocery and supply stores can empty in less than a day if there is a problem. Simple supplies can save lives, if on hand. People may not have what they want, but can have simple needs cared for even with minimal prep by local authorities. It should be obvious to intelligent informed people that you must be prepared to care for yourself.

There are several types of problems that preppers are trying to prepare for. Some are downright lunacy but others are very legitimate. The most obvious are financial collapse, disease, war or terrorist attack and natural disasters. All of which are very real possibilities, as noted by the news we see every day. How people cannot admit this is beyond me! Every day you will find people dismissing the obvious. If that makes them happy now, then good for them. Unfortunately, those are the ones that cause preppers to find a need for secrecy of their prepping activities. Unprepared people, by the hordes, will attack anything of value, should SHTF (The Sh*t Hits The Fan) happens. A common term used by preppers. Another one is WROL (Without Rule

Of Law). So when WROL and SHTF occurs, who will be ready, and who will be a target of those who are not.

In today's world of solar panels and wind up radios, why would anybody not have simple cheap obvious basic prepper supplies on hand, even if not an avid prepper. Even if you don't believe there will be a prepper type problem, a short power outage can cause an acute need for such basic supplies. The government has warned Americans several times how fragile our power system is, but some people just can't seem to get the hint. It should be obvious the government is stockpiling away more supplies than they could ever need under "Normal Emergency Conditions" and have been doing so for many years. However for some reason they don't seem to see the need for publicly known stockpiles that can be utilized by us. Could it be that they know something we don't and don't really care if nonessential personnel, such as us, will survive? Of course it could. Whats wrong with people who ignore the obvious, I may never know! Granted many people are going paycheck to paycheck or don't even have a job, but that's no excuse for not even being aware that it may be important to just know prepping matters. Better safe than sorry, right? It is surprising just how many people don't see the logic in such a simple phrase. Especially considering the obvious access to news that shows that statement to be true. Nowadays Putin keeps explaining about how he can use nuclear weapons anytime someone threatens his authority in the area, but somehow people don't hear it. We are finding excuses to go there and threaten resources and countries he obviously will defend at some point. Are people living in a shell? Can they not see the world is unstable? Preppers can see it! Whether they are prepping for these obvious reasons or something that just doesn't make sense, they will be the ones that have the best chance to survive.

That's why its no wonder billions of dollars every year are being spent on prepping in this country alone. It is amazingly easy to prep nowadays. Even if you live in an apartment, you can be a prepper. Some people think that only a bug out bag can be had by apartment dwellers. Not so, you can store years of extra freeze dried food in a spare room that you don't use. You can have a small window solar panel that can charge a battery for night light and other low consumption accessories. You can have a ceramic water filter, UV light and water tablets, to use to recycle water over and over without having to have a great deal of replacement water on hand, and a small amount of emergency medical supplies and pharmaceuticals on hand without using much space. The excuses to not be prepared just don't make sense. Prepping can also be very fun. The learning experience alone is worth the effort. Learning how to use a firearm and conserve resources is a valuable skill. The many products available to the prepper community forces one to learn and become aware of skills needed in everyday life. Skills that can be valuable in normal times as well as bad times. Even if bad times never come, it would be nice to have the skills and knowledge just in case WROL and SHTF occurs. Even if you don't have any supplies, but are very knowledgeable, you are valuable and worth protecting by others who do have the means and need you.

Chapter 1: Diet to eat to supercharge your immune system

Good nutrition is important in the proper functioning of your immune system. A diet that is high in useless calories can only help you gain more weight, making your body vulnerable to infections. It is also a known fact that obesity or being overweight can create a lot of health problems that can also bring trouble to your immune system. It might not be able to respond properly or immediately due to your unfit body.

When your immune system is down or not functioning well, you should avoid consuming alcohol and sugar. Microbes love sugar, so when you consume sugar you also feed the microbes and make them stronger. Your love for sugar only benefits the microbes in the end.

Your Ideal Diet

A diet full of vitamins and antioxidants can help boost your immune system to give your body the ability to fight off infection. Let the color of the fruits and vegetables guide you in choosing the kinds to take and include in your daily diet. Choose the colors dark green, orange, yellow, and red for your fruits and vegetables because the said colors are packed with antioxidants that your body needs.

You can try apples, citrus fruits, berries, kale, onions, carrots, spinach, red grapes, and sweet potatoes. Make sure to choose the fresh and organic ones. Commercially-grown produce usually contain chemicals, such as those in pesticide, that won't be washed away completely with water. When you eat produce that received chemical treatments, it is possible that the harmful chemicals can bring more damage to your body– even though you are eating what can be considered as healthy.

Other foods that have the ability to boost your immune system include fresh garlic and traditional chicken soup. Garlic is famous for its antiviral and antibiotic properties, and chicken soup has always been the number one choice of mothers to combat common cold or flu. Studies show that a steaming bowl of chicken soup eases the symptoms of cold and flu, and somehow gives comfort to the ailing body.

Fungi such as maitake, reichi, and shiitake mushrooms may help your body enhance the production of chemicals that can fight off infection.

Chapter 2: Top 25 fundamental foods to stockpile

Making a survival pantry is not that easy as it sounds. While preparing your pantry, you need to ensure that you have all the required food in proper amount for longer periods of time. Many people just believe in just filling the pantry with whatever things they feel like. They fill their pantry with all canned food, as they are suggested by the experts. However, these foods may not help you stay fit and healthy during an emergency or a disaster.

There are many foods that perish with time. You don't want to open a can of food, and you find it in bad condition. Your money is wasted plus it will be difficult for you to thrive. We bring you a collection of 25 items that can meet the requirement of your body, and can keep you fit and healthy during a disaster.

25 MUST HAVE SURVIVAL FOODS

With a list in your hand, you go to the supermarket to shop for your survival pantry. But, once you reach there, you are not sure which foods to select. The normal thing that you will do is buy foods that you and your family like. However, it is not certain that these foods will help you to keep health and fit during a disaster or emergency; There for, you need to be caution while buying foods for your survival pantry. These are 25 items that you should consider for your pantry to help you and your family survive a disaster.

1) Canned Foods: Canned foods are highly suggested for the survival pantry. They are manufactured in a way to last for months at a time. You can opt for canned fruits, canned vegetables, canned meats, and soups. All you need to keep in mind is to watch their manufacturing or expiry dates. Also, you need to maintain a rotation so that you get fresh canned food at the time of an emergency.

2) Dried Legumes: Dried Legumes like beans, peas, and lentils are low in coast and high in protein and fibber. There are many varieties of legumes to choose from. Try pinto beans for burrito or taco's, kidney beans for chilly, lintel for lintel soup or a bean mix for soup.

3) Crackers: Get different types of crackers not just saltines, include cheese crackers, gram crackers, thin wheat crackers, whole wheat crackers, and other flavour crackers. Gold fish shape crackers and animal crackers are always a hit with children. Varity pack are a great way to get a lot of different flavours at once.

4) Nuts: Nuts are a nutrient dense food which means that they are rich in nutrients for the number of calories contain in them. The FDA, Food and Drug Administration, suggest eating a ounce and one half or about a hand full of nuts daily. They can be a major source of energy and protein for your body. You need to stock a lot of nuts in your survival pantry. Walnuts, and peanuts are just a few that are available. Can mix nuts are a great way to get them all. Of course if anyone in your family is allergic to nuts don't include them in your survival pantry. This way, you will ensure that your family gets all the required nutrients even during emergency or disaster.

5) Peanut Butter: Peanut butter is another good option that you can consider for your survival pantry. It is a good source of protein and almost everyone loves it. Other nut butters such as almond butter, cashew butter, and hazel nut butter can provide variety in your diet during a emergency. Again, don't include peanut butters if someone in your family is allergic to nuts.

6) Pasta: Pasta can be part of a good diet. It's high in carbs. and very filling. Buy it in an assortment of shapes like shells, bowties, and tubes. Try whole grain pasta to maintain your intake of whole grains which contain fiber and essential minerals.

7) Pasta Sauce: If you are stocking pasta in your pantry don't forget the pasta sauce? Rather you buy it in a jar or make it from scratch, make sure to keep some in stock.

8) Flour: Flours like whole wheat and white has a long shelf life and is in the basics of many recopies. Flour manufactures recommend storing flour in a air tight container like a glass jar, plastic bag or plastic container

9) Seasonings: Most people don't want to eat unflavior, blan food. Store all your frequently used family favourites such as, salt and pepper, onion and garlic powder, chilli powder, and cumin, basil, and rosemary. As always, include what your family likes to eat

10) Sugar: Sugar is a group of carbs. that provide a quick and easy energy boost. But use sugar sparingly, the American Heart Association recommends no more than 100 to 150 cal. a day coming from added sugar. .

11) Bouillon Products: You all ready have can meat on your list, add bouillon cubes or powder for a easy and hot snack or a flavour boost in soups.

12) Kitchen Staples: Baking Soda, baking powder, vinegar, yeast, and similar kitchen staples are also necessary food items. Because they are so common in the kitchen, people forget about adding them to their survival pantry.

13) Honey: Honey has a long shelf life and has been use by humans for thousands of years as a sweetener and cough remedy. Also use for wounds and burn treatment buy medical grade honey for this use. Children under the age of 1 should not eat honey due to the risk of botulism.

14) Unsweetened cocoa powder and instant cocoa mix: Cocoa powder is very versatile and cocoa mixes have dried milk as a ingredient.

15) Pudding and Gelatine: Including pudding mixes as well as gelatine cups to minimize cooking and keep your kids happy.

16) Whole Grains: Include whole or instant oat, rice or barley in your pantry. Plain corn mill can be made into muffins. Grits plain or instant is another form of corn mill. Wheat berries can add variety to your grains.

17) Non-fat Dried Milk: Milk is an important part of your diet because it contains calcium, potassium, vitamin D, and protein. All these nutrients are necessary for healthy bones. The Unite States Department of Agriculture recommend 3 cup of mile per day starting at age 9 and continuing into adulthood. Children under age 9 need 2 -2 1/2 cups of milk per day. The USDA also suggest low fat or fat free milk.

18) Plant-based oil: Plant based oils, like olive oil, peanut oil, and vegetable oil have long shelf lives. Oils are fats that are liquid at room temperature. Oils add flavour to cook foods and are the main ingredient in salad dressing.

19) Breakfast Cereals: Breakfast is the most important meal of the day. Cold or instant hot breakfast cereals start the day right.

20) Seeds for sprouting: Sprouted seeds can provide fresh healthy food during an emergency. The most popular seeds for sprouting are alfalfa, water crust, and broccoli. Beet, lentil, and sunflower sprout are also tasty. Buy seeds meet for sprouting. Seed companies offer several varieties as a collection. Store the seeds in a sealed mason jar, and keep them dry and bug free. You might want to practice sprouting before an emergency so that you are familiar with the process.

21) Popcorn: Buy whole popcorn cornels instead of microwavable popcorn. Microwave popcorn is expensive on a cost per serving bases. Many brands are high in salt and use palm oil which is high in saturated fats.

22) Instant mash Potato: Instant mash potatoes are a easy and popular addition to any meal. Instant potato flakes come in a variety of flavours such as cheese, roasted garlic, sour cream and chive as well as plain.

23) Packaged meals: Can beef stew, can chilli, can pasta with sauce or packaged meals. Just heat and eat. What could be easier.

24) Drinking water: Drinking water needs and storage.

25) Fruit Juices: Can help as a supplement to water, and will provide nutrition and quick energy as well. Like can foods, check for expiration dates and rotate usage to maintain maximum freshness.

Listed above is a proper list of all must have foods in your survival pantry. You need to keep your family healthy and fit during emergencies. These must-have foods, you will be ensuring that your family stays strong, and is able to cope during tough time. All you need to do is calculate the amount of these foods for your requirement. Start collecting these for your survival pantry, today.

Chapter 3: What food you should buy

Kiwis

Can reduce the length of the common cold. Can also help reduce the risk of children getting sick. Kiwis have high levels of vitamin C, antioxidants, folate, and potassium. The whole fruit can be eaten, including the peel, which can triple the amount of fiber. The peel also contains a special prebiotic that can be highly beneficial to microbiomes. A study reviewed in the Canadian Journal of Physiology revealed how green and gold kiwi fruits can help improve immune functioning and even provide extra protection against the cold and flu (Stonehouse, Gammon, Beck, Conlon, Von Hurst, & Kruger, 2013). This study showed that since kiwi are high in vitamin C, E, and K as well as antioxidants that those in higher risk groups, such as children and older adults, consuming this fruit can help give extra support to the immune system to fight off infections will also reduce the severity of symptoms.

Blueberries and other berries

Berries contain vitamin C antioxidants that prevent inflammation and cell damage. They provide the body with a chemical known as anthocyanins, that can help prevent colds, urinary tract infections, and reduce high blood pressure. Blueberries contain a high amount of pterostilbene which helps boost the immune system naturally. A case study published in Molecular Nutrition and Food Research analyzed the compounds to boost immunity and found that the most impactful was pterostilbene (Robbins, 2018). Berries are a great addition to salads, oatmeal, and muffins or pancakes.

Broccoli and other Cruciferous Vegetables

A study performed on mice, led by Dr. Stockinger, showed that mice who ate cruciferous vegetables were able to better fight off intestinal pathogens ("Cruciferous vegetables help," 2017). Cruciferous vegetables are necessary for optimal immune system functioning. This includes foods like kale, collard greens, mustard greens, bok choy, broccoli, and brussels sprouts. Kale provides you with the most beneficial anti-inflammatory agents. They contain beta-carotene, vitamin C, E, and K, folate, lutein, and zeaxanthin. They also provide you with sulfur substances, glucosinolates, which makes a phytochemical that boosts the immune system and produces anti-cancer agents.

Ginger

Ginger is a powerful anti-inflammatory and antioxidant, that contains antimicrobial properties to defend against infectious diseases. Gingerol, found in ginger, gives it its anti-cancer properties. Ginger root can be easily found and stored in the freezer. There are also dried, powdered, and oil forms of ginger.

Green Tea

One of the most powerful teas around. It contains catechins, antioxidants, quercetin, and L-theanine, all of which effectively fight off viruses and infections (Robins, n.d.). It has even been shown that drinking green tea regularly can help reduce the risk of cancers (Robins, n.d.).

Aside from the foods mentioned above you should aim to include these superfoods into your diet as well.

- Matcha
- Kale
- Spinach
- Goji berries
- Elderberries
- Chia seeds
- Sunflower seeds
- Pumpkin seeds
- Yogurt
- Bell peppers
- Turmeric
- Cinnamon
- Almonds
- Citrus fruits
- Mushrooms
- Chickpeas
- Salmon
- Sardine

Foods That Hinder the Immune System

Fast foods aren't just bad for your waistline but eating greasy foods from most chain fast food places can negatively impact your health. This is because these foods, which are often high in sugar and low in fiber, which can reprogram the response of the immune system. Continually consuming these foods puts the immune system in high alert and it responds as though there is a constant threat. This constant high alert puts unnecessary stress on the immune system. And even when you switch to eating a healthier diet, and eliminate fast food, the immune system still stays on high alert which can cause negative health problems (Allen, n.d.).

Monosodium glutamate (MSG) can cause oxidative stress to the spleen and thymus, which affects lymphocytes, whose job is to remove foreign invaders from the body and to produce antibodies. The lymphocytes produced are typically fewer and function improperly, which can trigger an immune overreaction. Removing MSG from your diet can help reverse the negative effects over time (Allen, n.d.).

Alcohol reduces the function of macrophages, the cells that attack foreign invaders, throws off immunoglobulin and cytokine levels, can impair the production of T and B-cells, as well as disrupt Circadian rhythm or sleep cycles (Allen, n.d.).

Caffeine can boost cortisol levels which is a hormone released when feeling stressed. This can affect your mood and metabolism. T-cell production can also be reduced when consuming caffeine regularly, resulting in your lymphocytes being suppressed and interleukin production to lower (Allen, n.d.).

Aside from the foods mentioned above you should avoid these foods as much as possible.

- Coffee
- Energy drinks
- Diet Pop/Soda
- Fried foods
- Fast foods
- MSG food
- Alcohol
- Fruits and vegetables treated with pesticides
- Processed sugar
- Refined oils
- Additives
- Processed flour or Gluten

Foods to Avoid with an Autoimmune Disease

Those with an autoimmune disease can be more sensitive to certain foods. These foods can also worsen symptoms and can make the condition worsen at a more progressive rate. Those with an autoimmune disease will often follow a strict autoimmune diet which focuses on eating primarily fresh fruits and vegetables, as well as healthy fats and fish.

Foods that should be avoided when you have an autoimmune disease include:
- Caffeine
- Alcohol
- Sugar
- Grains
- Dairy
- Red meat

Artificial Sweeteners

Many people look for a sugar substitute to replace the everyday white processed sugar found in many homes. Artificial sweeteners are often thought to be better for your health, but they are synthetic sweeteners that are primarily made from chemicals and all-natural sources are processed out.

The most common artificial sweeteners are:

- Saccharin
- Aspartame
- Acesulfame potassium or Ace-K
- Sucralose
- Neotame

These are often considered a great alternative because most contain no calories and are used in a number of packages that claim to have "no sugar added." Artificial sweeteners have been linked to a number of health issues such as obesity (Casey, Obert, Pearlman, 2017) . This is primarily due to artificial sweeteners interfering with signals in the body. The way the brain responds to these sweeteners also changes. Because these sweeteners are not actually sugar, they also interfere with blood sugar levels and puts individuals at a higher risk for glucose intolerance (Chodosh,2018).

Environmental Risks

It was thought that genes and age often determined who was susceptible to a disease more, but now it is believed that the environment has a bigger impact. Environmental factors such as dust and air pollutants can trigger someone already at higher risk for disease to become ill. Respiratory infections are becoming prominent, resulting in death across the globe.

When babies and young children are exposed to these harmful environmental factors early in life, they become less resistant to diseases. Early exposure to air pollutants like cigarette smoke, pesticides, and pollution disrupt the proper development and functioning of the immune system. This can cause the immune system to be unable to identify harmful pathogens that enter the body or cause it to over-react to pathogens that should be considered harmless. While symptoms may not be present in the first years of life, many individuals who are exposed early on to harmful chemicals and toxins in their environment are more likely to develop cancer or other immune deficiencies.

How can you help reduce the risk of environmental factors on your immune system?

1. Avoid using products that contain harmful chemicals in your homes. Instead use baking soda and vinegar as a daily cleaner which is just as effective yet, less harmful.
2. Keep all heating and cooling ducts clean. Dust particles can stay in vents and turn into airborne irritants. Performing a yearly cleaning on your home's vents can

reduce the number of irritants in your home.

3. Use air filters to remove irritants and pollutants from your home. You can also add air purifying plants to your home such as aloe vera, peace lily, spider plant, boston fern, or areca palms.

4. Using a water filtration or purifying system can also help reduce the risk of bacteria or harmful toxins that may be in your water systems.

Chapter 4: Top 10 foods to fight disease & improve immune system

Although every family's food pantry is going to look a little different, there are some fundamentals that you should know. Check out the following list and make it a priority to get these items into your survival pantry first.

1. Rice

Rice is a prepping staple. It is filling and you can eat it plain or add it into soups and casseroles for a little more sustenance. A little goes a long way. A 50-pound bag holds about 500 servings!

2. Beans

Go for a variety of pinto, kidney and navy beans. Buy 50-pound bags of each. Beans are high in protein and very filling.

3. Oats

A bag of oats is cheap and it will go a long way in making sure your family's bellies are full. Oats are another excellent addition to stews and soups. You can buy buckets of oats that will last for 25 years or more in your pantry.

4. Canned meat

You may not be a fan of Spam today, but when there isn't a butcher or a meat market, you will be thrilled to get some meat into your diet. Invest in cans of tuna, chicken and fish as well.

5. Canned fruit

Choose a variety of fruits that your family will eat. Do yourself a favor and avoid buying the large, commercial cans. If you can't eat it in one setting, it will end up going to waste. You may not have a refrigerator to put the leftovers in.

6. Canned veggies

Buy veggies your family currently eats today. Make sure you have a large variety to keep things interesting.

7. Canned soups

These are great for those quick meals when you can't go through the process of preparing a meal from scratch. Choose low sodium varieties when you can. You don't need the extra salt in your diet at a time when water is in short supply because salt makes you thirsty.

8. Flour

Flour will be a staple. You will have to make your own bread, rolls and cakes. You can also use it to thicken soups and stews. You will want to store at least 50 pounds. Make sure you store it in the freezer for 2 weeks before you add it to your food pantry to kill off weevil eggs.

9. Instant potatoes

Again, a little water transforms a box of potatoes flakes into a delicious meal. Store some powdered gravy mixes to really jazz up your meal.

10. Pastas

Store a variety of pastas i.e. spaghetti noodles, macaroni noodles and linguine are all good starting points. Pasta is cheap and makes for a quick and easy meal.

These are just basic staples. You can buy a variety of freeze-dried foods as well. However, these tend to be a little pricier. You can get complete meals in a can. It is important to keep in mind that the recommended serving sizes are rather small. A single serving will likely not be enough to satisfy an adult.

Diversify the food you put on your shelves to keep you and your family from suffering from food fatigue. Food fatigue can cause serious digestive issues and occurs when you eat the same thing all the time. Your body needs a variety of proteins, fibers, fruits, veggies and carbohydrates in order to function at its best.

If your kids have a particular snack they like, it is a good idea to load up on it. You want to help them maintain a semblance of normalcy. Providing them with their normal bedtime snack or afternoon snack will go a long way to making them feel comfortable and relaxed.

Chapter 5: The best foods to focus and tips to store them for long time

There are several factors that you'll need to take into consideration before learning how to store different kinds of foods.

The first factor to take into account for storing food is humidity. If you have too much humidity in general, especially when it occurs with the other factors we'll discus, it can cause many long lasting foods to go bad. This includes cereal, crackers, and flours. These foods are known for being long lasting, but with too much humidity, they'll stale and become bad for eating. Other shorter lasting foods, such as meat and potatoes, will be in even worse shape: they'll rot.

Another key factor to take into consideration for food storage is light. Almost all foods, especially beverages and spices, will last longer in dark and cool conditions with limited light.

Perhaps the single most important factor in food preservation in general is temperature. A few foods can easily cope with changes in temperatures, but most foods cannot. As a result, you will need to control the temperature in the environment these foods are kept in.

For instance, the typical freezer temperature is around zero degrees Fahrenheit, while the typical temperature in a standard refrigerator is between thirty and forty degrees. But the foods stay well preserved in these conditions because the temperature is controlled. In a grid down emergency situation, it's likely there will no power meaning there is very limited time left for the foods in your freezer and your refrigerator.

What does this mean? When stockpiling food for an emergency, store food where you can control the temperature of the environment you will be putting the food in without a power source. This means if you're planning on stockpiling food that you require a refrigerator or a freezer for, you should strongly reconsider your stockpiling strategy.

Also important is the types of containers and wraps that you store your food in, such as plastic containers, glass containers, plastic bags, plastic wraps, and aluminum foil. Each of these have their pros and cons. For example, you can use glass containers and aluminum foil to heat up food over a fire or in a makeshift oven. Plastic bags are also more convenient than some solid bags, because they can be arranged and stored in position that solid bags can not fit in.

Another danger to your food storage is infestation. Rodents, insects, microorganisms, mold, and anything else similar can get into the food and make it go bad very quickly. Not only can pests eat the actual food, they can also contaminate it and make it hugely unsafe to eat or drink. You should utilize proper storage and package conditions to prevent infestation. Even better, you can store your food in an environment that invasive critters typically don't like. It is impossible for all aerobic organisms to survive in an environment that is oxygen free. In addition, rodents and most other animals are not capable of chewing through plastic containers in a short amount of time, and they certainly can't bite their way through metal containers.

Next, we'll talk about moisture, and the bottom line is that the less moisture is in your food the better off it will be. The reason for this is because more moisture encourages the growth of dangerous bacteria and other harmful organisms. Foods that are stored in metal and glass will better protect the food against moisture. High levels of humidity like we discussed earlier will also be a key player in encouraging moisture developing in your food. Condensation likes to build up in most cans or metal containers in high humidity areas, and usually where there is a drastic change in temperature. As a general rule of thumb, you will want to check your cans and storage containers often to check for any sign of condensation or moisture.

Oxygen is another factor of food storage to take into account. An environment with higher oxygen will encourage oxidation...and you'll definitely notice oxidation if it occurs. Oxidation leads to powerful odors, rancidity, and discoloration in foods, but even if you're desperate enough to eat food that smells and looks like that anyway, the nutritional value of that food will have decreased substantially.

With that in mind, you will want to create an environment for your food with as low of oxygen levels as possible. Without oxygen, insects and other aerobic organisms are unable to survive, as they are oxygen dependent organisms. In low humidity conditions, whole grain foods and beans will be the best foods to store as they both have natural oxygen barriers and are great for storing for long periods.

Finally, it's also important about how you handle the food when you store it. Rough handling can deal damage to the food in addition to compromising the strength of the container: containers can break, crack, or tear. The seams that the lid twists or latches onto can also become twisted or broken, which would allow oxygen to seep into the container and drastically decrease the shelf life.

Chapter 6: Dietary basics for a strong immune system

In addition to the tips from the preceding chapter, here are important guidelines that you can refer to at home to further improve your immune system.

Include the following ingredients in your menu planning:

- Garlic—promotes activity of white blood cells. Eat it raw for a more potent effect.

- Onion—breaks up mucus and increases blood circulation. Include generous amounts in salads uncooked for better effects.

- Ginger—acts as an inflammatory substance and good for flu. You can turn it into hot tea to help ease sore throat.

- Olive oil—helps in providing good fat to your body so that cells can grow properly.

- Pepper—promotes growth of white blood cells. It helps you sweat, helping in the function of your immune system.

- Ginseng—is commonly believed to enhance the immune system, although more conclusive studies will yet confirm this claim.

- Aloe vera—has been helpful in treating burns and minor wounds.

- Pure honey bee—has been used in helping the immune system treat colds, and sore throat.

These natural products are used locally to strengthen—not only the immune system—but the whole body as well. They have anti-microbial and healing properties, and can be safely ingested. They are also inexpensive. Be sure to check for allergies to stay safe.

Instruct family members to observe proper hygiene.

Common sense dictates that you have to be clean to avoid acquiring infection. Observe proper hygiene by taking a bath daily, brushing your teeth at least twice a day, and washing your hands before and after meals. It's universally established that washing the hands with soap and water frequently is the best way to prevent infection.

Create an awareness of this healthy habit within your family. Of course, you can always include other people in your noble intention. Your end-goal is to stay uninfected and well. When you maintain your health, you also help your immune system to develop properly. Staying healthy will improve your immune system in the long run.

On the other hand, don't be afraid to expose your children to the environment. Allow them to play outside amidst the grass, dirt or soil, so their bodies can develop some antibodies on their own. A clean countryside is a good place to do this, not in a slimy, dirty and polluted neighborhood.

Decide wisely. If there's potential danger of contracting pathological diseases, then refrain from exposing them. You would not leave your children playing in a clean stream, if you know that malaria abounds in that area. Likewise, you will not allow your them to play in a gutter that can be infected with H-fever mosquito vectors.

Get a regular dose of early morning sunshine

Expose yourself to early morning sunshine for a healthy dose of Vitamin D. These are the light rays that are gentle to your skin. You can do this when the sun is still starting to rise on the horizon and its rays are not hot. This can be around 6 to 7:30 am. Don't go beyond that because too much sun exposure can lead to skin cancer.

Early sunshine activates the precursor of your vitamin D so that it can be converted into an active form. This activated vitamin D promotes skin health, thereby, improving your immune system. Remember that your skin is one of the components of your immune system, being your first line of defense.

Take good care of your skin

It goes without saying that you have to take good care of your skin and ensure that it's clean. You can use light moisturizers to prevent dryness and irritation. Treat skin sores and wounds promptly so they do not get infected. If you have diabetes mellitus, work with your doctor to manage the condition and promote better wound healing.

Cry, if you must

Have you ever wondered why you feel better after crying? This is because tears cleanse the eyes in addition to releasing pent up emotions. Tears wash away microbes from your eyes so don't hold back your tears. Cry whenever you feel like it.

Make love regularly

Yes, Virginia, making love regularly can help improve your immune system. There's a scientific connection that researchers were able to establish. An immunoglobulin, particularly salivary IgA, was found to increase in production in people who made love more. The immunoglobulins, are antibodies, and therefore part of your immune system. Nurture a pet

If you're alone at home, consider caring for a pet. Developing a bond with a pet can bring peace and relaxation for you. This will reduce your stress and help improve your immune system, as it does when you socialize.

Strengthen family bonds

Your immune system improves when you have strong family ties. It's because stress is greatly reduced within your home. When stress is reduced and managed, your immune system improves, as well. This has something to do with the stress hormones, glucocorticoids, and IgG.

These are home guides that you can implement to improve your immune system. Continue to build on this list with natural and safe activities that make you feel light and worry free as you progress on your journey to a stronger immune system.

Chapter 7: Tips for prepping for survival

Creating a survival pantry is definitely a big job. However, there are plenty of people who have made it a true art form. You can learn a lot from other people's experiences. There is no need for you to try and reinvent the wheel. Save yourself a lot of time, money and frustration by learning from other people's successes and failures.

The following are some of the most useful tips, tricks and hacks you can use when it comes to managing your own food and water and making it last as long as possible. When it comes times to dip into your survival food pantry, you want to do what you can to make it last.

- Buy a book about edible plants in the wild. Foraging is one way you can supplement your food pantry in a survival situation. It is difficult to remember the characteristics of every single edible plant. Keep a book on hand that includes pictures so you can be sure.

- Learn how to hunt today so you are proficient at it when you need to harvest an animal for survival. Fresh meat will supplement the staples you have stored in your pantry.

- Eat the food in your refrigerator first before you turn to your emergency food storage. The food in the fridge and freezer will spoil within a day if it isn't consumed. This adds another day to your food supply. Some of the food in the freezer could be dried in the sun to preserve it.

• Invest in Mylar bags to store your dried foods in. Mylar bags block light and oxygen and can extend the shelf life of many of your foods. Place the sealed Mylar bags inside 5-gallon buckets with lids to keep out pests.

• Build rain catchment systems today to prepare for the day when you won't have access to running water. A gutter and downspout are all you need to harness the rain and fill up an entire 55-gallon rain barrel in a single storm.

• Disconnect your water heater from the main water line as soon as disaster strikes. This is one way to keep the water in the tank clean and uncontaminated from outside sources. Most water heaters hold about 50 gallons of water, which can keep your family alive for a week or more.

• Plan on doing most of your manual labor during the coolest hours of the day in the summer to cut down on your need for water. Working in the heat of the day will cause you to need more water.

Chapter 8: Food storage

For this chapter, we will discuss some specific foods that you can store for six months or more.

Vegetables

- For vegetables, you will want to store them under the driest conditions possible. However, different types of vegetables hold different characteristics. For instance, carrots and potatoes are naturally dry while tomatoes have more fluids in them. As a result, the temperatures and storage conditions will vary slightly. So what is the answer to storing different vegetables in the same place?

- The answer is a root cellar. A cellar has cool temperatures and limited humidity, which is perfect for storing most vegetables for a long time. Lettuce stored in these conditions can last you for two to three months, squash can last two to three years, and other root vegetables can last several years as well. Specific types of vegetables that you can store in these conditions include ginger, potatoes, onions, beets, and squash. While each vegetable will require a different plan in order to be stored properly and with the most longevity without a freezer or a refrigerator, the point is that they all at least require similar treatments like we just discussed.

Grain

- Grain is another important food to store for the long term. This includes flour, rice, cornmeal, and millet. These should be stored in tightly sealed containers to prevent moisture; just a small hint of moisture will be all that's needed to contaminate the grain. Historically speaking, glass containers have been most commonly used to store grain, but recently, plastic containers have come to fulfill this role as well.

- While many people store their grain in grain sacks, this method is largely ineffective. It's very easy for mold to develop in sacks, and pests such as insects and rodents can easily work their way through the bag material to get to the grain, consuming much of it and infecting the rest. It only takes two to three days for grain to spoil when on the ground or when moisture sets in. To test grain to see if it's still good and safe to eat, see if it can sprout. Grains sprouting under the right conditions should take up to a week. If the grain fails to sprout, discard all of the other grain that was in the same container.

Herbs and Spices

- You may not think of herbs and spices as being a critical food to store for the long term; after all, how are you supposed to live off of just pure herbs and spices? Well, you can't. But you can still add herbs and spices to your other food to add much flavor. Even in an emergency grid down situation in desperate times, you can still add good taste to your foods. Beyond that, they will be very valuable items when it comes to bartering with other groups. Even better, is how easy and convenient it is to store them. They are commonly sold in prepackaging, that make it very easy to be stored in a normal pantry. You can plan on storing herbs and spices for between six months to one year; after that time, they will gradually start to lose their flavor. This is because the oils in the herbs and spices that give them their flavor will start to evaporate after prolonged use.

Meats

- Having enough protein in your body is absolutely necessary for survival, and there is no better source of protein in foods than meat. But the problem with storing meat is that it's tricky. Unpreserved meat has an extremely short life span, and must be refrigerated, frozen, dried, cured, or smoked with no questions asked. Since it can be complex to keep meat adequately preserved so that it is has a long storage life and is good enough quality to eat, the types of techniques used for this vary. Fortunately, you will soon learn what these techniques are.

- One common technique used for meat storage is the dry ageing technique, which will tenderize the meat for over three weeks. An even more long lasting method than this is to dry the meat. Drying meats has been used by humans for thousands of years and is just as commonly used today. As long as you have a heat source, you can store dried meat outside of refrigeration in a secure environment at normal temperatures because there is limited moisture inside of the meat. This prevents the meat's chances of being spoiled due to microbial organisms.

- Open air drying of meats has also been used for centuries and is commonly used today. However, there is a major risk with this method, because the meat will be exposed to outside materials that can contaminate it: debris, animals, and so forth.

- Finally, you can also always 'salt' the meat. Salt, when in high concentration, is very adept at drawing the moisture out from the membranes in meat. This process is called 'osmosis'; you might have heard that term in biology or chemistry class in high school and/or college. Bacteria spoils meat, and unfortunately, it's also very effective at it. But bacteria also needs water to survive and if you can remove the water by salting, it's impossible for the bacteria to gain a foothold.

- We'll learn about all of these food storage and preservation methods and more in later chapters.

Oils

- It's pretty difficult to cook something without oil, so as a result, this is definitely something that you will want to stock up on. The most common kind of oil found in the grocery store is olive oil, and while it is undoubtedly great for cooking, it's also very easy for it to go bad. Even so, some olive oils have been known to hold their nutritional value for up to two years. Alternative oils that you can stock up on include virgin oils, which have the most nutritional value, and coconut oils, which are very heat stable and are low to oxidize. In other words, coconut oils will stay good and nutritional much longer than olive oil can.

Coffee and Tea

- You may have thought that a cup of hot coffee or tea in the morning is something that you would have to sacrifice in an emergency grid down situation, but this is far from the truth. Tea has been around for several millennia; historically, it has been used to make poor quality water taste better and to kill bacteria when it was boiled. You can easily apply the same set of skills to you and your family in a grid down scenario. In addition, coffee has some certain health benefits as well: it can raise mental alertness, but even better, a cup of hot coffee in the morning will certainly serve as a valuable morale booster.

- Teas have a number of health benefits that you can utilize in a survival situation: they have a very calming effect on an individual, and they also lower the risk of developing blood clots or higher levels of cholesterol. Tea is also a natural remedy for the common cold as well. Due to these beneficial health properties in coffee and tea, you would be wise to include them as part of your food storage.

Flour

- Wheat is a very basic food that also happens to be nutritious: it's one of the few food sources that's armed to the teeth with protein, fiber, minerals, and vitamins all at the same time. Wheat flour is therefore a very vital food source to stock up on in the pantry. When stored in its original container under the right conditions, wheat flour is very long lasting and won't go bad for up to six months.

Corn, Rice and Cereals

- Finally, there's corn, rice, and cereals. We're putting these foods together because the storage conditions for all three are very similar and they are drastically important to store. All three of these foods are very long lasting, and have high levels of Vitamin E and fiber. What's even better, is that you can store all three of these things in bulk. You can have literally entire sealed buckets filled up with corn, rice, and cereals. An unopened box of cereal can last up to eight months when stored in a dark and cool environment; rice can last up to six months, and frozen corn can last up to a year, with a shelf life of about a week after it has been thawed. The bottom line is with corn, you can stockpile it in your freezer for a long time, but if your power goes out, you'll want to eat as much of the corn as you can right away.

Chapter 9: Preppers pantry

By now you know what survival pantry is, why you need it, and how you can plan for your short and long term emergencies. Now, in this chapter you will learn about the 10 necessary steps that will help you store your survival pantry. Stocking survival pantry can be a tough job if not done properly. You need to ensure that you have stored every necessary thing in your panty as per your requirement. Let us have a look at these 10 steps.

Step 1: Store Water

We have discussed that water is as essential as food. Generally, people pay attention to food and forget about water. Getting drinkable water during any emergency or disaster gets difficult. It is not easy to survive without water. Without water, you won't be able to live beyond three days. Hence, the first thing you should do is keep water at the top of the survival pantry checklist. On an average, a person needs a gallon of water for a day. You need to plan accordingly. If you are planning for long term emergencies then you need to include more water for other important things like brushing and washing.

Step 2: Buy Canned Food

Anytime, canned foods are good for survival pantry. While making a list for your survival pantry, make a list of canned foods that your family loves. Along with canned foods, include crackers, nut butter, pasta, rice, protein bars, and dried fruits. Canned and packed foods have a longer shelf life plus are rich in nutrients. These foods can be an importance source of energy during emergencies. It is suggested that you collect all your favourite canned foods and snacks so that you don't regret it later.

Step3: Stock and Rotate

Disaster or emergency will not strike soon you have to ensure that foods of your survival pantry are fresh. This is why you need to keep your survival pantry foods in rotation. Firstly, you need to look for a proper place in your kitchen where you can stock all these foods of your choice. Secondly, you need to arrange for a rotation of these stocked foods. Rotation is important as this way you can keep your survival pantry stocked with fresh foods. Survival pantry is not all about stocking food. It is about stocking fresh foods that can survive for longer time. In your stock pantry, you keep the fresh items at the back and old item in the front. Consume from this stock pantry, but fill it back immediately so that none of the item is missing during emergency. This way, you can keep your survival pantry with fresh required items.

Step 4: Add Freeze Dried Foods

Canned foods have an expiry date. They last for a year or two. If you stock your survival pantry only with canned foods then you might incur loss. While stocking foods for survival pantry, include freeze dried foods as well. The reason being, these have a life of around 25 years. So, once you have stocked your survival pantry with this, you are relaxed. Stocking freeze dried food will allow you to enjoy a variety of item during emergency.

Step 5: Bulk Buying

Buying in bulk is the most economical thing to do. When you buy in bulk, you can expect some discounts. Some make a mistake of not buying in bulk. These people end up spending more on the survival pantry then needed. Due to this, they tend to neglect the survival pantry. However, when you buy in bulk, you save money; which means, you don't find survival pantry as a burden on your pockets and you tend to continue with it with an ease.

Step 6: Survival Kitchen

During the short term emergency, you can survive on canned foods. However, you need to also prepare yourself for the long term emergencies. It is necessary that you keep your survival pantry equipped with important kitchen equipment. Keep cooking stove, fuel, matchsticks, utilises, and other necessary kitchen things in your pantry. You need to be prepared for the bad and the worst.

Step 7: Canning and Dehydrating

If you are preparing your survival pantry then you should know about canning and dehydration. It is a process by which your foods are fresh for longer period. This technique is not known to many. By canning and dehydrating these foods, you keep them in proper amount of oxygen, which is essential to keep them fresh. There are certain ways by which you can keep them fresh. These are:

a) You can keep dry items in a jar that absorbs oxygen.

b) Select food grade buckets for larger quantities. These buckets are made up of special plastic that is free from toxins.

c) You can keep your items in the mason jar by zapping out all the air.

d) You can also opt for oven canning.

Step 8: Food to Fight Fatigue

During disaster, it is quite normal to get fatigue. You need to include foods that will help you fight this fatigue. There are various foods that can be essential for your survival pantry. These foods are bacon, canned butter, coconut oil, bakery food, cheese, coffee, breakfast freeze dried food, desserts, canned meat, and Mexican food. Include all these in your survival pantry if you want to survive through the emergency.

Step 9: Grow Your Own

There is no certainty that you will get fruits and vegetables during short or long term emergencies. Also, it can be hard to imagine living without them. This is because they are rich in nutrients. Though, you will have canned veggies, but fresh has their own charm. It is suggested that you learn to grow them. There are a variety of vegetables that you can grow in your backyard or in containers. Once you learn to grow your own veggies, you are prepared for the disaster.

Step 10: Keep Food in Safe Place

This is the last and the most important part of the step. You need to keep your food in safe place. It is necessary that you get range of containers and keep different foods in these containers. For your ease, you can label these containers. This will save a lot of time while looking for certain things. Plus, it will be easy for you to keep a track of all these items while you are rotating them.

The above mentioned 10 steps are essential for survival pantry. Following these steps will ensure that you get everything in your survival pantry and at right amount. If you don't follow these steps, then there are chances that you can miss out on various things. Having a survival pantry is essential, but when you have a proper survival pantry, you ensure to save your family from starving and provide them all necessary nutrients that they require. Make a check list and start with your survival pantry.

Conclusion

The information on the immune system as presented here is vital to understanding how to strengthen the defense system against sickness. We tried to present it in a straightforward and simple way so that you and your family members (even the younger ones) can refer to this book at any time.

Utilize the recommended methods in this book properly and you will definitely improve your immune system and your health in general. Health is wealth and you have to put in time and effort in order to reap the benefits of a healthy body. Nothing good will happen unless you act on the information you got from this book.

It's important to note that there are a few techniques that should be implemented carefully, because the opposite can happen if the step is not followed correctly. You're encouraged to go back and double check the information in the various chapters, should you have doubts.

Don't miss out!

Visit the website below and you can sign up to receive emails whenever Mary White publishes a new book. There's no charge and no obligation.

https://books2read.com/r/B-A-PIZP-LYLRB

BOOKS2READ

Connecting independent readers to independent writers.

9 798201 495435